IT'S SCIENCE!

Growing up

Sally Hewitt

W

FRANKLIN WATTS
LONDON • SYDNEY

First published in 1998 by Franklin Watts
Paperback edition 2001

Franklin Watts
96 Leonard Street
London EC2A 4XD

Franklin Watts Australia
56 O'Riordan Street
Alexandria, Sydney
NSW 2015

Series editor: Rachel Cooke
Designer: Mo Choy
Picture research: Alex Young
Photography: Ray Moller unless otherwise acknowledged
Series consultant: Sally Nanknivell-Aston

ISBN 0 7496 3067 1 (hbk.); 0 7496 4270 X (pbk.)

Dewey Decimal Classification Number 612.6

A CIP catalogue record for this book is available from the
British Library.

Printed in Malaysia

Acknowledgements:
Bruce Coleman pp. 7tr (Kim Taylor), 7bl (Jorg and Petra Wegner), 14 (Jane Burton), 16l (M.R. Phicton), 17t (Fritz Prenzel),
19cl (Dr. Eckart Pott), 20l (Jane Burton), 20r (Jane Burton); FLPA pp. 17b (Silvestris), 23t (Brake/Sunset);
Sally and Richard Greenhill p. 25t; Robert Harding pp. 10tr; Image Bank p. 24; NHPA pp. 7br (Daniel Heuclin), 22r
(Daniel Heuclin), 23b (Nigel J. Dennis); Oxford Scientific Films pp. 15t (Reed Williams), 15b (M.Wilding), 18 (Mike Birkhead),
19tl (Mike Birkhead), 21tl (Breck P. Kent), 21tc (Rudie H. Kruiter), 21tr (Rudie H. Kruiter), 21bl (Rudie H. Kruiter),
21br (John Mitchell), 22bl (Z. Leszcznski); Photofusion pp. 6l (Reen Pilikington), 12 (Clarissa Leahy);
Planet Earth Pictures pp. 16r (Frank Krahmer), 19bl (Frank Krahmer), 19tr (Margaret Welby);
Stock Market pp. 8tl, 8br, 10l, 10br, 11tl, 11bl, 13. All other photography commissioned by Franklin Watts.
With thanks to our model, James Moller.

IT'S SCIENCE:

Growing up

Contents

Born today!

This tiny baby has just been born.
When you were a baby like this one, you couldn't do much for yourself.
You needed an **adult** to feed you and keep you safe, clean and warm.

Young **human** beings have to be looked after by their **parents** for a long time. As we grow up, we learn to do more and more things for ourselves.

THINK ABOUT IT!

Find a picture of yourself as a baby. In what ways do you look different? How much have you grown? What can you do now that you couldn't do then?

Some newly-born or newly-hatched creatures have to be able to do more for themselves straight away than others.

A baby bird must be fed. It has to grow feathers and learn to fly before it can leave the nest.

A young snake slithers away and survives by itself as soon as it **hatches** from its egg.

A baby deer has to walk as soon as it is born so that it can keep up with the **herd**. Its mother still feeds it, though.

Growing up

Human beings like you take many years to grow up. They need grown-ups to care for them, to give them food and a safe place to live.

Tina is a new baby. She has no teeth. She needs her mother's milk, which she sucks from her mother's breast. Some babies drink milk from a bottle.

Sarah is thirty. She is grown up and has a baby of her own. We call a fully-grown person an adult.

John is one. He has grown some teeth and can eat all kinds of good food to help him grow strong and healthy. He still likes milk, but now he drinks cow's milk and has it in a cup.

Lee is fifteen. He is a **teenager**. He is almost grown up.

Ali is two. He can walk by himself. He has longer legs and more hair than John. What other differences tell you he is older?

Aaron is nine. He already has his grown-up teeth. His baby teeth fell out when he was about six.

TRY IT OUT!

Have you got photographs of yourself on some of your birthdays?
If you have, put them in order of age.
Beside a picture of you on your last birthday, write your height, the size of your feet, how much you weigh and the date.
Keep a record of you – growing up.

Learning

You are growing all the time. You will stop growing when you are grown up, but you will never stop learning.

Babies begin to learn about the world around them as soon as they are born.

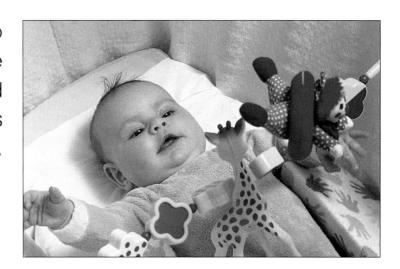

Toddlers learn to walk and talk.

When you go to school, you learn to read and write, to do sums, and all kinds of new things.

As you grow older, you learn to do more complicated things. You do not need as much help from other people.

Many teenagers leave home to do a job or go to university.

💡 THINK ABOUT IT!

When you are grown up, you will learn to do a job and earn money for the things you need. What job would you like to do? Why would you like to do it?

A new baby

Did you know you began life as an **egg** about the size of a dot?

A new life begins when a tiny **sperm** from a father joins an egg from a mother. The egg starts to grow inside the mother's womb.

A mother's **womb** is a safe place for a baby to grow until it is ready to be born. You can sometimes feel the baby moving about.

Find your tummy button. It is the place where a tube joined you to your mother when you were growing in her womb. The tube supplied you with food and **oxygen**.

It takes about nine months for the tiny egg to grow into a baby that is ready to leave the safety of its mother's womb and live in the world outside.

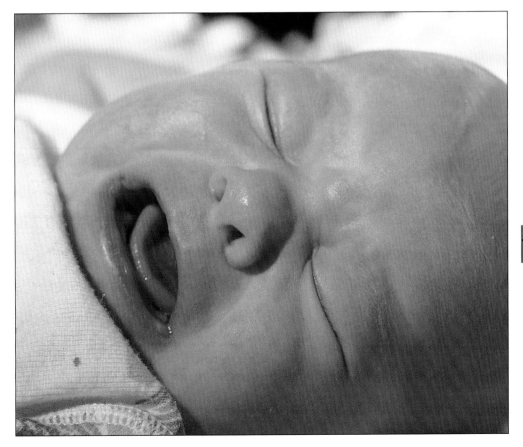

As soon as the baby is born, it takes its first breath of air and often cries very loudly!

 **LOOK AGAIN**

Look again at page 8 to find out what this new-born baby's first meal will be.

13

Cats and kittens

A mother cat has about four to six kittens. They grow inside her for eight weeks. They are blind, deaf and helpless when they are born.

Like the babies of humans and other **mammals**, kittens drink their mother's milk. Their mother feeds them and looks after them until they can go hunting on their own.

THINK ABOUT IT!

Pet cats don't look after themselves completely even when they are fully grown. What would you have to do to look after a pet cat?

Have you ever watched kittens play together?
They are learning how to become fierce hunters and to look after themselves. A cat is fully grown and can have kittens of its own before it is a year old.

 **LOOK AGAIN**

Look again at pages 8 and 9. How much more growing and learning does a one-year-old baby still have to do?

15

Pouches

Baby kangaroos have a very unusual place to grow before they are ready to look after themselves – in a pocket!

A tiny baby kangaroo, called a joey, is only 2.5cm long when it is born. It crawls into its mother's pocket which we call a pouch.

It stays in the pouch and sucks milk for about 6 months, until it is big enough to jump out and look for its own food.

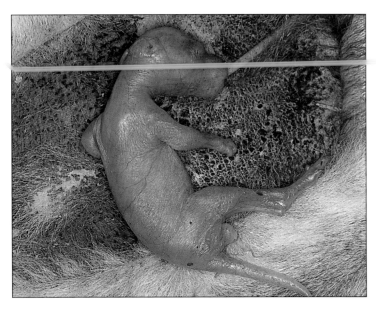

 **TRY IT OUT!**

Find a ruler and draw a line 2.5 cm long. Now you can see how tiny a joey is when it is born.

Kangaroos, koala bears and wombats are all a type of animal called a **marsupial**. Marsupials have pouches for their babies to grow in.

Mother koalas carry their babies in their pouches as they climb through the trees.

Wombats are diggers. Can you see why it is a good thing their pouches open backwards?

 **THINK ABOUT IT!**

Human adults pick their babies up in their arms. What other ways have you seen adults carrying their babies around?

Swans and cygnets

You grew inside your mother's womb. Marsupials grow in their mother's womb and then in her pouch.

All baby birds grow inside an egg laid by their mothers. Eggs are packed full of the food and goodness a chick needs to grow.

This mother swan is sitting on her eggs to keep them warm and safe.

LOOK AGAIN

Look again at page 13 to find how you were fed when you were growing inside your mother.

When there is no more food left in the egg, the new swan is ready to hatch.

It takes a day for the baby swan to tap open the egg and struggle out.

A baby swan is called a **cygnet**. When the cygnet is two days old, it is ready to swim.

A cygnet has different feathers from an adult swan. Its beautiful white feathers will grow when it is about 2 years old.

🔆 THINK ABOUT IT!

Birds build nests where they lay their eggs and look after their chicks. The nest keeps them warm and safe. What makes your home a good place for you to grow up?

Amazing changes

Amazing changes happen to some creatures as they grow.

These two pictures are of the same type of animal –
an **insect** called a stag beetle.

A stag beetle hatches out from its
egg as a soft-bodied **larva**.

Later, it changes to become a
fierce-looking adult stag beetle.

 **TRY IT OUT!**

Make a list of all the things that are different between a stag beetle
larva and an adult stag beetle. Now make a list of the all things
that are the same.

A butterfly goes through amazing changes as it grows up, too.

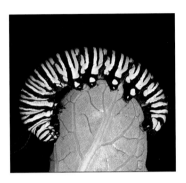

A butterfly lays its eggs on a leaf.

The eggs hatch into caterpillars which start to munch the leaves.

At the beginning of the summer, the caterpillar hangs on a twig and becomes a **chrysalis**. Inside the chrysalis, amazing changes take place. The caterpillar is turning into a butterfly!

When the butterfly is fully formed, it struggles out of the chrysalis, spreads its wings to dry and flies away.

Butterflies are the grown-ups. They lay eggs on a leaf and a new life begins.

Reptiles

Most **reptiles** lay eggs. They have different ways of making sure the eggs are kept safe and warm. They grow up in different ways, too.

A female python lays about 100 eggs. She coils her long body around her eggs to make a warm, safe nest.

Snakes grow quickly when they are young. They never stop growing completely until they die.

As snakes get bigger, they grow a new layer of skin and leave the old one behind.

 **THINK ABOUT IT!**

Very few people live to be as old as a hundred. How old is the oldest person you know?

A female crocodile digs a hole in the river bank for her eggs and covers them with sand.

Crocodile parents guard their eggs to keep them safe from enemies hunting for eggs to eat.

When the baby crocodiles hatch, the mother scrapes away the sand and carries them in her mouth to the river.

Giant Nile crocodiles live for a very long time. It is thought that some of them live to a hundred years old!

Growing old

Human beings stop growing in height, but we keep changing as we get older.

Emily is three, her mother is twenty-nine, her **grandmother** is fifty-five and her **great-grandmother** is eighty.

Look at the differences between Emily, her mother, her grandmother and her great-grandmother. How do people change as they get older?

☼ THINK ABOUT IT!

All living things die – animals, plants and people. Sometimes people die when they are young because they are ill or have an accident. Most people live a long time and die when they are old.

Sam and his granddad enjoy talking together.
Granddad is sixty-five, so he can teach Sam a lot
of the things he has learnt over many years.

 **TRY IT OUT!**

Play a matching game. Ask your family,
teachers and friends for photographs of
themselves as babies and young children.
Pin them up. Can you tell who is who?

The cycle of life

When a new animal is born it becomes part of a **life cycle**. At the end of its life, it dies, but new young animals are born and start new life cycles.

Follow the circle round to find the life cycle of a salmon.

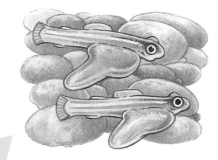

When a baby salmon hatches, it is 2.5 cm long. At first, it feeds off its egg yolk, which it carries with it.

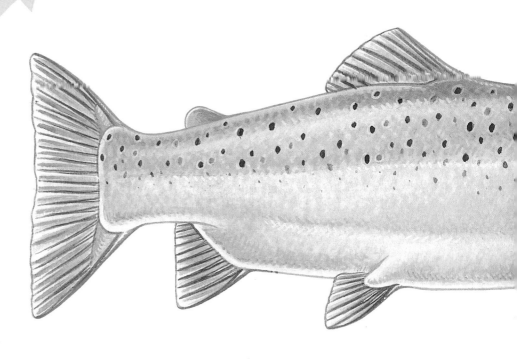

The salmon lays its eggs near the same place it hatched.

The adult salmon finds its way back to the river it came from and swims up it.

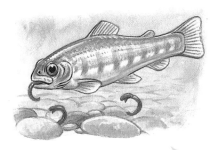

The baby salmon starts to feed on small river creatures. It grows quickly.

After 2 years, the salmon is about 18 cm long. It swims down the river to the ocean.

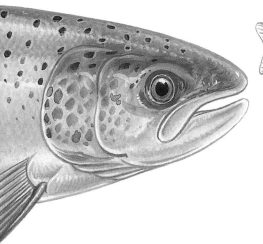

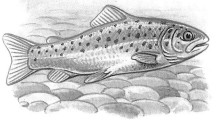

The salmon lives and feeds in the ocean. It grows even more – an adult weighs at least 4.5 kilograms.

 **TRY IT OUT!**

Draw the life cycle of a frog. You need to draw pictures in a circle of frogspawn, tadpoles, a froglet and an adult frog. Join the pictures up with curving arrows. Try drawing a life cycle of another creature that is in this book.

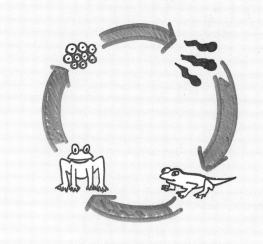

Useful words

Adult A person or animal becomes an adult when they are fully grown.

Chrysalis All butterflies and moths become a chrysalis while they are changing from a caterpillar to an adult butterfly.

Cygnet A cygnet is a young swan.

Egg People and animals start life in an egg. Some animals, including people, keep the egg inside their bodies until the baby inside is ready to be born. Other animals, like birds and most reptiles, lay eggs and the baby animals later hatch from these.

Grandmother Your grandmother is your mother's mother or your father's mother. Your grandfather is your mother's father or your father's father.

Great-grandmother Your great-grandmother is the mother of your grandfather or grandmother.

Hatch When a baby animal hatches, it breaks out of the egg and begins its life in the outside world. Baby chicks hatch from birds' eggs.

Herd Grass-eating animals such as deer live together and move around feeding in groups called herds.

Human You are a human. All people – men, women, boys and girls – belong to a group of animals called humans. Humans are mammals.

Insect Insects are a group of animals with no backbone. Their bodies are divided in to 3 parts and protected by a hard case. They have 6 legs.

Larva Most insects hatch from an egg as a larva. (More than one larva are called larvae.) Larvae usually look quite different from the adults they grow into. For example, a caterpillar is the larva of a butterfly.

Life cycle Every new born animal becomes part of a life cycle. It is born, grows up and has babies of its own, starting new life cycles, before it dies.

Mammals Mammals are a group of animals with backbones. They have some hair or fur. Baby mammals drink milk from their mothers.

Marsupials Marsupials are a group of mammals that have pouches or pockets for their babies to grow in. Kangaroos, koalas and wombats are all marsupials.

Oxygen Oxygen is a kind of gas that is part of the air we breathe. Our bodies need oxygen to work.

Parent A parent is a mother or father.

Reptiles Reptiles are a group of animals with backbones with scaly, waterproof skin. They breathe air. Some live on land and others in water.

Sperm Sperm is the seed from a father. When a sperm joins an egg from a mother, a new baby begins.

Teenager A teenager is a person aged between thirteen and nineteen – the numbers that end in 'teen'.

Womb Baby humans and other baby mammals grow inside their mother's womb until they are born.

Index

About this book

Children are natural scientists. They learn by touching and feeling, noticing, asking questions and trying things out for themselves. The books in the *It's Science!* series are designed for the way children learn. Familiar objects are used as starting points for further learning. *Growing up* starts with a new baby and explores human and animal growth.

Each double page spread introduces a new topic, such as learning. Information is given, questions asked and activities suggested that encourage children to make discoveries and develop new ideas for themselves. Look out for these panels throughout the book:

TRY IT OUT! indicates a simple activity, using safe materials, that proves or explores a point.
THINK ABOUT IT! indicates a question inspired by the information on the page but which points the reader to areas not covered by the book.
LOOK AGAIN introduces a cross-referencing activity which links themes and facts through the book.

Encourage children not to take the familiar world for granted. Point things out, ask questions and enjoy making scientific discoveries together.